ATHENA: THE GODDESS WITH THE GRAY EYES

Mythology and Folklore
Children's Greek & Roman Books

BABY PROFESSOR
EDUCATION KIDS

Speedy Publishing LLC

40 E. Main St. #1156

Newark, DE 19711

www.speedypublishing.com

Copyright 2017

ATHENA was known in Greek Mythology as the goddess of courage, wisdom, and crafts. Her symbols were the serpent, the owl, the spear, the shield, the olive tree, and armor. Zeus was her father and Metis was her mother. Her Roman name was Minerva. She lived on top of Mount Olympus. In this book, you will be learning about this beautiful goddess with the gray eyes.

Athena is one of the Twelve Olympians and is well-known as being the patron god of Athens. She also assisted several Greek heroes including Odysseus and Hercules on their travels and adventures.

HOW WAS ATHENA TYPICALLY DEPICTED?

Athena was typically pictured to be a warrior goddess who was armed with a shield, helmet, and spears. Occasionally she would be shown wearing a shield or a cloak that would be adorned with the head of a monster named Medusa.

What Were Her Skills and Powers?

Like the other Olympians, she was immortal and could not die. She was great at war strategy and providing the heroes with courage, as well as being one of the wisest and most intelligent of the Greek gods.

ATHENA

CHARIOTS

Included in her special powers was her ability to invent crafts and items. Athena invented the plow, rake, ship, as well as the chariot. In addition, she created several of the skills that were useful to women of Ancient Greece, including weaving and pottery.

Athena's Birth

The god Zeus, who was leader over the Olympians, was her father, and a Titan by the name of Metis was her mother. Even though Metis was the wife of Zeus, he was fearful of her power. He heard of a prophesy that one of her children would overtake his throne and promptly swallowed Metis. He now believed this problem to be solved.

ZEUS

Little did Zeus know, Metis was pregnant carrying Athena at the time he swallowed her. Athena was born inside of Zeus and she created the shield, spear, and helmet. As she continued to grow inside Zeus' head, he started to have a horrible headache. He eventually could not take the headache any longer and instructed the god Hephaestus to crack his head open using an ax. Athena proceeded to jump out of his head. She was already full-grown, and armed with the spear and the shield.

ATHENA THE PROTECTOR

After winning a contest against Poseidon, she was now the patron goddess of Athens. Each of the gods would present Athens with a gift. Athena created the olive tree and presented it to Athens and Poseidon created the horse and presented it to the city. The people of Athens found both of these gifts useful, but believed that the olive tree would be more valuable and Athena was named their patron.

PARTHENON TEMPLE

Athena was honored by the construction of a large acropolis that was built in the city's center. A gorgeous temple called Parthenon was built atop the acropolis in her honor.

ASSISTING THE HEROES

In Greek mythology, Athena is known for helping the heroes in their travels and adventures by helping Hercules to achieve his twelve labors, Perseus to figure the best way to defeat Medusa, Odysseus with his Odyssey adventures, and helped Jason build his magical ship called Argo.

PERSEUS HOLDING HEAD OF MEDUSA

ARACHNE

ARACHNE

Athena was the inventor of weaving and became known as the best weaver in Greek mythology. However, Arachne, who was a shepherd's daughter, claimed that she was best weaver throughout the world. Athena became angered and she visited Arachne, challenging her to a contest. Once the contest started, Athena wove a picture showing how gods would punish the mortals for claiming to be equal. Arachne proceeded to weave a picture showing how gods would interfere and play with lives of the mortals.

Once the contest was finished, Athena became angry when she looked at Arachne's work. It was not only better than hers, but it also made the gods appear foolish. Athena cursed her and proceeded to turn Arachne into a spider.

ATHENA'S TITLES

Because of her beautiful gray eyes, Athena was sometimes referred to as "gray eyes". She also had the titles of "goddess of council", "protector of the city", and "Pallas".

GREEK MYTHOLOGY

There were many gods surrounding the many myths and stories about the Greeks. Greek mythology is built around the tales and stories of the Greek gods, the goddesses, and the heroes. In addition, it is the Ancient Greek religion as they would build temples and would make sacrifices to the major gods.

The Greek gods consisted of the Titans, the Olympians, and the Heroes.

The original (elder) gods were known as the Titans. There were 12 Titans, including the parents of Rhea, Cronus, and Zeus and they ruled during the golden age. Led by Zeus, they were overtaken by their children.

MOUNT OLYMPUS

There were 12 Olympian gods and they were known as the major gods, residing on Mount Olympus.

A man considered brave and strong was known as a Greek hero and was preferred by the gods. They would accomplish brave adventures and exploits. Even as a mortal, a hero seemed to be related to the gods.

HERODION THEATER, ATHENS GREECE

THE CITY OF ATHENS

nown to be one of the greatest cities around the world, Athens became the center of science, art, philosophy, and power around the world during the time of Ancient Greece. It is also one the world's oldest cities, with its history going back more than 3400 years. Athens is the heart of the civilization of Ancient Greece as well as the birthplace of democracy.

Athens is named for Athena, the Greek goddess, who was goddess of war, wisdom, and civilization as well as holding the title "patron of the city of Athens". The Parthenon, which is a shrine to her, sits atop a hill located in the city's center.

ANCIENT AGORA OF ATHENS

THE AGORA

Ancient Athens' center for government and commerce was known as the agora. There was an open area which was used for meetings and was surrounded by several buildings. Some buildings were temples, including temples that had been built to honor Apollo, Hephaestus, and Zeus. Some of these buildings were government facilities, including the Mint, where they made coins, as well as the Strategeion, where Athens' military leaders, known as the Strategoi, would meet.

This became a meeting place for people to hold discussions about their ideas regarding government and philosophy. This is where their democracy started.

ACROPOLIS OF ATHENS

THE ACROPOLIS

Constructed on hill in the middle of Athens was the Acropolis. Surrounded with walls made of stones, it was originally built as a citadel and fortress where people could go once they were attacked. Many buildings and temples were later constructed overlooking Athens. However, it continued to be used as a fortress.

RUINS OF THE TEMPLE OF ATHENA

The Parthenon, a building dedicated to Athena, was a building in the center of the Acropolis. This building was used for storing gold, as well. The Temple of Athena and Nike, as well as the Erchtheum, were also located at the Acropolis.

THEATER OF DIONYSUS

ocated on the Acropolis slope were theatres where festivals, as well as plays, would be celebrated. The largest theatre was the Theatre of Dionysus, who was patron of theatre and god of wine. They would hold competitions to find out who wrote the best play. The design of the theatre was so great that 25,000 people could attend and everyone would still be able to hear and see the play.

THE AGE OF PERICLES

The Age of Pericles occurred from 461 to 429 B.C. when the city had reached its peak under the leadership of Pericles. Pericles was promoting democracy, literature, and the arts during this era. Additionally, he constructed several of the city's tremendous structures, which including construction of the Parthenon and rebuilding the Acropolis.

STATUE OF PERICLES

STATUE OF ALEXANDER THE GREAT

ANCIENT GREECE

Dominating most of the Mediterranean over a thousand years ago was Ancient Greece. It was at its peak when under rule of Alexander the Great, who ruled most of Europe as well as Western Asia. The Romans followed the Greeks, and most of Roman culture was greatly influenced by the Greeks.

Most of the foundation for today's Western culture was formed by Ancient Greece, including philosophy, government, art, mathematics, science, sports, as well as literature.

TRAVELER IN THE ACROPOLIS

STATUE OF HOMER

ANCIENT GREECE TIME PERIODS

Historians have often divided up Ancient Greece history into three time periods:

ARCHAIC PERIOD – The Archaic Period took place from the beginning of Greek civilization in 800 B.C. until Democracy was introduced in 508 B.C. Also occurring during this time period was Homer's writing of The Odyssey and the Illiad as well as the beginning of the Olympic Games.

CLASSICAL PERIOD – The Classical Period is what we typically think of as Ancient Greece. They saw the rise of amazing philosophers such as Plato and Socrates and Athens was now governed under a democracy. The end of this era ended in 323 B.C., with the rise and death of Alexander the Great.

STATUES OF PLATO AND SOCRATES

HELLENISTIC PERIOD - The Hellenistic Period started with the death of Alexander the Great until Rome was able to conquer Greece in 146 B.C. The word Hellenistic stems from a Greek term "hellens" which is the name that Greeks called themselves.

Athena – Greek Goddess of Wisdom and War

Athena was one of the many goddesses that was endowed with great prowess on warfare and wisdom. She gave courage and inspiration to many heroes in Greek history. She was an amazing and beautiful goddess.

There are many more myths and tales surrounding her life. For additional information about Athena, as well as the other gods and goddesses of Ancient Greece, you can visit your local library, research the internet, and ask questions of your teachers, family and friends.

Visit

BABY PROFESSOR
EDUCATION KIDS

www.BabyProfessorBooks.com
to download Free Baby Professor eBooks
and view our catalog of new and exciting
Children's Books